THE MONEY PSA

A BIBLICAL FRAMEWORK TO
RESET YOUR PERSPECTIVE,
SPIRIT, AND ACTIONS

MAYA MCNEESE-HARGETT

The views expressed in this work are solely those of the author and do not necessarily reflect the views of the publisher, and the publisher disclaims any responsibility for them. Furthermore, acknowledging the dynamic nature of the internet, it should be noted that any web addresses or links in this book may have changed since publication and, consequently, may no longer be valid.

ISBN: 979-8-9889561-0-5
eISBN: 979-8-9889561-1-2

Printed in the United States of America

Cover Design: Taofeek Abdulqoyum Abiola
Photo: Lisa Wilder Baker (wildershots.com)
Editor: Faith L. Okoro (Ed.)
For more information and additional resources, please visit:
www.hersequoiaconsulting.com

DEDICATION

To all who seek to honor God in their finances.
To my family, whose love and support fuels my passion
to provide biblical financial guidance.

ACKNOWLEDGMENT

Victory Church (Norcross, GA) opened my mind to the concept of biblical financial stewardship. The entire Money + Wisdom team and all the students and clients I served have colored my perspective and activated this calling.

Special thanks to James and Sharon Vincent, who seamlessly pushed me past my introverted tendencies, and to Chris and Sarah Martin for preparing our first budget and being great examples of how wonderful living without debt could be. These relationships were instrumental in building my biblical financial perspective.

I could not have completed this book without the support of my husband, daughter, and mother. Their unconditional love and strong belief in my capability to influence others have fueled my self-confidence and compelled me to speak my truth.

May you be blessed by something you read in this book.

TABLE OF CONTENTS

INTRODUCTION

Welcome to a new perspective on achieving personal financial success. I applaud you for investing in your financial future. I desire that the perspectives in this book will break the chains of unproductive financial behaviors and form bonds that heal and empower.

This is not the first book written on how to achieve financial success. However, this work fills the gaps between receiving biblical financial instruction and the full transition to a new fiscal lifestyle. When I experienced the benefits of victory over consumer debt, I was compelled to share the principles I've learned. Living with minimal stress and worry and without the burden of how to navigate a financial emergency has been life-changing.

I want you to sit comfortably when deciding on your next vehicle purchase, home purchase, and intentional income adjustment. I want you to have the tools to not just get out of debt but stay out of debt. This involves acknowledging that maintaining your debt freedom takes spiritual and practical discipline. You can win by addressing your financial convictions and tapping into a deeper spiritual connection with God.

Over the past ten years, my husband and I have dedicated ourselves to our church's financial ministry. We started as passive consumers of information and quickly became biblical financial advocates, and then stewardship ambassadors. We've directly and indirectly helped hundreds of people become more enlightened on Godly financial principles. Our participation in these activities obligated us to address our finances (otherwise, we wouldn't be living out the principles we were teaching).

Before and during our marriage, we amassed $195,000 in debt (67% of our debt was attributed to student loans). The accountability that comes with living out the principles you teach led us to pay off all our consumer debt in approximately 5 years.

While reaching this milestone was a blessing, we quickly realized our journey was far from over. Our celebration was quickly replaced with the sober reminder that debt would visit our household again if we did not figure out how to plan for future financial endeavors. So with the data we had from coaching others through their financial journeys, I began to compare the financial levers and circumstances that led to success and contrast them with the factors that typically resulted in missing the mark.

Once we read and understood what God has to say about our finances, we realized that we had to be "all in," committing our minds, spirits, and actions to living a debt-free lifestyle. Scripture makes it plain. We chose to dedicate ourselves to a financial discipleship walk, holding ourselves to a higher standard than the world. We had to navigate through strongholds, delayed gratification, accountability partners, and several other factors. These things helped us to change our perspective and our relationship with money.

We despise debt because it hinders us from fully living our God-given purpose. We honor and are obedient to God through tithing. We practice honesty and integrity in our financial dealings. The Lord has blessed us to purchase two vehicles with cash, to have provisions to fund our daughter's college education without using any debt, and to begin building an investment portfolio.

I hope this book accelerates your own financial discipleship journey so that you will reach financial success and be free to live out your God-given purpose. Every moment of delay also delays the Kingdom's impact. Start applying these principles today, and God will honor your obedience. Your faith will increase, and God will begin to enlarge your territory.

Isaiah 55:6-11 NIV

⁶ Seek the Lord while he may be found; call on him while he is near.⁷ Let the wicked forsake their ways and the unrighteous their thoughts. Let them turn to the Lord, and he will have mercy on them, and to our God, for he will freely pardon.⁸ "For my thoughts are not your thoughts, neither are your ways my ways," declares the Lord.⁹ "As the heavens are higher than the earth, so are my ways higher than your ways and my thoughts than your thoughts.¹⁰ As the rain and the snow come down from heaven, and do not return to it without watering the earth and making it bud and flourish, so that it yields seed for the sower and bread for the eater,¹¹ so is my word that goes out from my mouth: It will not return to me empty, but will accomplish what I desire and achieve the purpose for which I sent it.

THE FRAMEWORK

I've learned that perfecting your biblical financial stewardship walk can be encompassed within a simple framework: Changing Your **P**erspective, Healing Your **S**pirit, and Deploying the Right **A**ctions. The Perspective-Spirit-Actions (PSA) method ensures you have effectively explored and solidified all aspects of your financial life, and this comprehensibility facilitates financial success.

In Chapters 1-4, we will explore your **PERSPECTIVE** to ensure a bigger purpose and a greater goal that stimulates you. This will involve goal planning, self-evaluation, discipline, and discipleship.

In Chapters 5 and 6, we will explore your **SPIRIT** to break down your strongholds and build up the character necessary to navigate tough times. The spiritual aspect of financial stewardship involves prayer, self-awareness, accountability, and faith.

Lastly, in chapters 7-10, we will explore your **ACTIONS** to ensure you formulate better habits to prepare you for a dynamic world. Let's get started!

FRAMEWORK: A real or conceptual structure intended to serve as a support or guide for the building or something more valuable.

CHAPTER

1

DEFINE YOUR WHY

GAIN CLARITY ON YOUR PURPOSE.

First things first, it's important to know why you are doing something. For this content to be meaningful to you, it's important to know why you want to be debt free – why you want to achieve financial success. The awareness of your foundational motivation will sustain you on your financial marathon. Be prepared to be inundated with conflicting requests for your time and money, your precious resources. You can make better decisions when you rely on your definition of utopia.

We once experienced a couple who wanted to go on a mission trip. Their "why" was to impact God's kingdom through physical, personal connections and needs-based missions across the globe. They needed enough financial freedom to leave their normal commitments and responsibilities for weeks to go on that mission trip.

Many people who desire to be more active in missions are held back by their financial situation. The average person working a traditional job cannot afford to be without a steady income or paycheck for very long. They typically also have debt or financial commitments to creditors that would default if the paychecks stopped coming. Once you add the mission trip expenses into the equation, the desire to help others through missions can seem daunting.

This couple needed to get themselves out of debt. Being on the mission field was a calling for them, something that motivated them to keep moving toward the future. They applied the concepts we will discuss in this book and spent 18 months paying off all the necessary debt and gathering the funds to complete the trip. They accelerated their timetable because they were motivated to execute what God called them to do.

LESSON: Defining your why creates a rallying point, something you can share with a like-minded community and leverage to sustain your journey.

To define your why:

1. **Fast to clear your spirit (2 Corinthians 3:17)**
   Take a break from your normal routine—abstain or significantly reduce the things that hinder you from being able to think clearly. During this time, seek the Lord. Come to Him with a clear heart—ask for forgiveness for your sins. Stop listening to competing voices. Ask him for inspiration and clarity.

   Hearing from the Lord is important because it gives you boldness and clarity. It gives you passion, fuels it, and can speak to you in multiple ways. God may direct you through scripture, speak to you through others, provide you with a dream or a vision, or place you in particular circumstances that will enhance your clarity. For you to hear from God, you are going to have to stop and focus on his voice today.

When you define your "why," it should be kingdom-driven (Luke 12:15). If you are conceiving thoughts of selfish ambition, God may not speak to you during this exercise. However, be honest with God. He knows the desires of your heart, and He can help to change your character when it is your heart's true desire.

2. Be open to trial and error

Whether you receive full revelation in step one or not, there may be more than one interpretation for your inspiration. Try an alternate way if the first practical application of your why does not succeed.

3. Educate yourself

Educate yourself on creating definition, purpose, and clarity in your mind and spirit. Applying the mechanics of these principles will serve you well, so be prepared to invest time in these concepts.

4. Consult your community of trusted advisors

Utilize resources that help you find practical ways to hear from God. He may place people in your path who can speak to your journey. The information they provide may compel you to slightly modify your actions.

Financial decisions are (and will continue to be) a significant function of your existence – finances are connected to everything you do. Gain clarity on your purpose. That purpose will boost your motivation and bring you a few steps closer to being financially successful. Consider why God has uniquely placed you in this world at this time. Consider why He has called you to have your current level of provision. Ponder on how he wants you to impact the world. God will honor the desires of your heart when you remain focused on pleasing Him.

Download the **Define Your Why** worksheet to map out your thoughts.

BIBLE REFERENCES AND REFLECTIONS:

Matthew 6:16-21 NIV

[16] "When you fast, do not look somber as the hypocrites do, for they disfigure their faces to show others they are fasting. Truly I tell you, they have received their reward in full. [17] But when you fast, put oil on your head and wash your face, [18] so that it will not be obvious to others that you are fasting, but only to your Father, who is unseen; and your Father, who sees what is done in secret, will reward you. [19] "Do not store up for yourselves treasures on earth, where moths and vermin destroy, and where thieves break in and steal. [20] But store up for yourselves treasures in heaven, where moths and vermin do not destroy, and where thieves do not break in and steal. [21] For where your treasure is, there your heart will be also.

1 Timothy 6:17-19 NIV

[17] Command those who are rich in this present world not to be arrogant nor to put their hope in wealth, which is so uncertain, but to put their hope in God, who richly provides us with everything for our enjoyment. [18] Command them to do good, to be rich in good deeds, and to be generous and willing to share. [19] In this way, they will lay up treasure for themselves as a firm foundation for the coming age so that they may take hold of the life that is truly life.

CHAPTER

2

PLAN YOUR GOALS

INTENTIONALITY LEADS TO PROGRESS
AND RESULTS.

My husband and I have intentional, regular conversations about our goals. We align on our short, mid, and long-term family goals. These goals are then related back to our finances. This activity ensures there is no ambiguity in our financial relationship. Make no mistake, these can sometimes be difficult conversations (even today), but we recognize the importance of agreement and focus and how this recurring alignment facilitates a healthy marriage. We write down our financial goals, check them off upon completion, and adjust our timelines when things don't materialize as planned.

To plan goals, we must verbalize what we want and desire. A best practice is to also document why we desire those things. If the Lord has spoken to you, you have a responsibility to document his plans plainly (Habakkuk 2). We defined our why in Chapter 1, which will likely incorporate something we innately have within ourselves. Ideally, we leverage our skills to accomplish goals that will benefit the kingdom. Use your "whys" to inform and develop practical, bite-sized milestones that will be your guiding tool.

If you're new to this activity, begin with brainstorming. A good brainstorming session will document several possible ways to accomplish your purpose. When brainstorming, try to identify at least ten possibilities without discounting practicality. Be creative and outlandish—complete this activity in a space that encourages freedom. If an idea is generated, write it down. This step is important because we don't want to lose any great notions.

Once the brainstorming is complete, it is time to identify your prioritization scale and then prioritize your ideas. Your prioritization scale could include many factors like effort, impact, value, urgency, or importance. Be consistent in your ranking scale. You could choose to rank your ideas in sequential order by each factor, or you could choose to score your ideas by each factor. Sequential order may be more tedious (especially if you are married and considering two opinions), but it is a quick way to solidify your preferences. Choosing the scoring method could result in a tie, but it could also provide more insight into why a particular idea should be further explored. Be cognizant that the different methods may cause different goals to rise to the top. Weigh the pros and cons of each method and choose your preferred way accordingly.

LESSON: Goal planning provides focus, prevents conflict (either in your own head or with your partner), and shows you that your goals are attainable.

Write down your goals and refer to them often. Once you have your goals, you can apply strategies, prayer, and supplication. God knows how to escalate and elevate your purpose and sometimes shorten the timeframe of when certain goals can be accomplished. So be sure to invite Him into the conversation.

To activate goal planning:

1. Download the *Goal Planning* worksheet to document and prioritize your plans.

2. Allocate time at least once a month to review your financial goals.

3. Be specific and clear on how these things will impact your short and long-term experiences. If there's a cost associated with your goal, which most likely there is, then capture the cost as well. If God has given you that vision, He will also give you the provision to execute it.

4. Be flexible when reviewing your goals, especially if you have someone else to whom you need to be accountable.

5. Go the extra step and schedule your goal-planning sessions on your calendar for the next quarter.

BIBLE REFERENCES AND REFLECTIONS:

Intentionality leads to progress and results. There's power in setting goals as a call to action. Take a moment to schedule a day each month to plan your goals.

Psalm 33:11 NIV

But the plans of the Lord stand firm forever, the purposes of his heart through all generations.

CHAPTER

3

EVALUATE YOUR HABITS, YOUR PERSONALITY, AND TENDENCIES

WE IDENTIFY OUR BLINDSPOTS SO WE CAN
ADJUST OUR DECISIONS ACCORDINGLY.

My husband and I have been married for 21 years. He is a spender, and I am a saver. More specifically, my shopping tendencies are more goal-oriented, whereas his shopping tendencies surround helping others. People with servant hearts find it difficult to say "no" to people. When they're in a store, and a salesperson makes a reasonable suggestion, they're more likely to make a purchase. From a different perspective, you could be someone who's always looking for high quality, deploying comparison and analysis to justify a purchase. This person could easily be persuaded to spend more on a purchase than needed. In either situation, too much of one tendency is ultimately not optimal. Ideally, we identify our blindspots so we can adjust our decisions accordingly.

Once we identified our differences, my husband and I had to navigate harmonizing our different spending behaviors and understand that it is not a deal-breaker when we want to make purchases for different reasons. Leveraging our goal-setting exercises as input, we set a particular amount that can be used on purchases in every spending category. Then, we adjusted our tendencies to fit within those boundaries. While this is a simplistic recipe for success, sometimes we miss the mark. When this happens, we give ourselves grace—counterbalances are possible. When we analyzed the decisions that make us stronger and those that don't add value to our lives, we concluded that change is needed.

In every marriage, if you are more of a spender, avoid walking down every aisle in the grocery or retail store. You are more likely to find something interesting and add that item to your purchase unexpectedly (also known as an impulse buy). Practical ways to counterbalance impulsive spending include reducing the number of trips to the store, making a list and sticking to it, and ordering your items online, which reduces "window shopping." These boundaries can help adjust your habits.

This concept of spending is important because it is culturally acceptable and encourages you to extend your finances well beyond your means. This premise is in direct conflict with what God desires. Yes, spending is inevitable, but how do you differentiate yourself from others and promote your faith if your spending behaviors resemble those who do not believe in God? The principles described in Romans 12:1-2 apply to your finances as well. Accomplishing your God-given goals through your finances likely involves changing the way you think. When you change the way you think, it will change your actions. When you change your actions, you will get a different result.

Before we go any further, figuring out your financial personality is important. Once you know your financial personality, you are more capable of identifying when those habits make appearances. Then, you must set strategies to avoid those particular tendencies. Once you've set the strategy, you can achieve victory over those detrimental routines. You have to identify your thoughts to change them, and once you've changed them, you will see that your results will move toward what you desire.

LESSON: Honestly evaluate your behaviors. Compromise (if you have a spouse or partner). Change the way you think (and it will change your actions). Perfection is not expected—give yourself grace and space to improve.

To gain victory in this area:

1. Determine your financial personality.
2. Examine the circumstances that surround unproductive habits showing up in your life.
   a. What are your earliest recollections of money? How did money impact your family's trajectory?
   b. Did your family plan for future purchases?

    c. Have you received an inheritance? If so, how has it impacted your life?

    d. Are you a faithful tither?

    e. What values are you teaching your children (or other young people in your extended family) about money?

3. Set strategies to avoid those tendencies.

I encourage you to take the **DISC Assessment** and then review the **Spending Behavior Matrix** to understand what spending attributes are common for your personality type. This information will provide direction to cultivate better behaviors.

BIBLE REFERENCE AND REFLECTION:

Romans 12:1-2 NLT

[1] *And so, dear brothers and sisters,[a] I plead with you to give your bodies to God because of all he has done for you. Let them be a living and holy sacrifice—the kind he will find acceptable. This is truly the way to worship him.[b]* [2] *Don't copy the behavior and customs of this world, but let God transform you into a new person by changing the way you think. Then you will learn to know God's will for you, which is good and pleasing and perfect.*

"Do the best you can until you know better. Then, when you know better, do better."

– Maya Angelou

CHAPTER

4

DISCIPLINE AND FINANCIAL DISCIPLESHIP

IN A MULTITUDE OF COUNSELORS,
THERE IS WISDOM.

If you're reading this book, chances are you've been exposed to other financial leaders who promote debt freedom. I also advocate for debt freedom. However, from my vantage point, the role of discipline, specifically spiritual and financial discipleship, cannot be over-emphasized if you want to maintain the debt freedom status. In your journey, you should have a financial mentor and coach you can approach when your upcoming financial decisions are unclear.

Marvin and Johnette sought our coaching when they were looking to purchase a home. They had recently completed a significant financial milestone - completely paying off their consumer debt. After accomplishing this milestone, they wanted to continue making wise financial decisions.

U.S. banks use a formula that typically results in lenders being approved for larger mortgage payments than they can practically afford if they seek to effectively allocate spending to all important areas of their lives. As this family navigated the housing market for the perfect home, they did so with the mindset of purchasing a home at the top of their price range. Eventually, through prayer, discernment, and practical budgeting scenarios, we helped them realize that spending too much on a mortgage would prevent them from meeting other goals and supporting their families.

Because we had worked with them for some time, they also had a list of short-, mid-, and long-term goals to consider. The couple has young children, and it is reasonable to assume that funds will likely be needed in the immediate future to support the children's activities or the children's education. We helped them see the importance of keeping their household expenses within a specific range so they could retain more income for access to other things. We assured them that God would honor their discipline in this area and that they would experience no lack in making a more kingdom-driven decision.

This recommendation was difficult for them to absorb because it didn't align with their way and timing (refer back to Romans 12:2). They ultimately purchased a beautiful, spacious home with a comfortable mortgage payment that enabled flexibility in their finances. They trusted our counsel, and we continued encouraging them at every step. We adore observing their family prosper and how they continue to please God in many ways.

If you're like me, you want to please God—to be a great disciple. We want our actions to be pleasing to Him. We want to do what God has called us to do. But, to be more effective in this area, we must have someone who can help us realize when we may be stepping outside of God's will or see when God may have a better plan for us than the one we have designed for ourselves. This person will be our accountability partner, someone who can bring biblical financial mentoring into our life so that we can stay on the path God has created for us.

Beyond an accountability partner, we need to begin to digest more of God's plan. There is accountability in scripture if you memorize and apply certain verses or passages of the Bible. Scripture gives you orientation. It gives you motivation. It gives you precision. It is gratifying to know that whenever you speak God's word and walk out its precepts, you will know that you are walking in God's purpose.

LESSON: You must figure out what's blocking you from being able to implement wise counsel. Better financial decisions are made in collaboration with a financial coach or mentor.

You will make better financial decisions when you:

1. Regularly check in with a coach or mentor. Like the couple in our example, their interactions with a financial coach changed their financial trajectory.

2. Are humble. The couple in our example above were humble and open to receiving correction and guidance from someone else. They were also diligent in implementing the recommended new habit or behavior. Sometimes, we ignore God when He speaks because we don't want to do what he suggests.

3. Implement and practice developing new habits, remembering that it takes time to master new habits (grace is abundant).

God will put others in your life to benefit you. In a multitude of counselors, there is wisdom. Visit our website to complete the **Schedule Your Consultation Checklist** and to learn more about our financial counseling services that will help you get back on track.

BIBLE REFERENCE AND REFLECTION:

Proverbs 12:15 NKJV

The way of a fool is right in his own eyes, but he who heeds counsel is wise.

CHAPTER

5

PRAYER

WHEN WE GIVE OUR CONTROL TO GOD,
HE CRAFTS BETTER OUTCOMES THAN
WE COULD HAVE IMAGINED OURSELVES.

Prayer is a primary method used to hear from God. Prayer is essential on this journey. When we pray to God, He provides us the guidance and clarity for the next steps and the decisions we need to make. John 10:27 says, *"My sheep hear My voice, and I know them, and they follow Me."* You can only hear God's voice if you listen to what He is saying through prayer and meditation. If you invite Him into the conversation, God can and will direct your financial decisions.

There is power in prayer. I often invite those in my trusted community to petition the Lord on my behalf (and they do the same). We also pray in small groups because the Bible says, "For w*here two or three are gathered together in My name, I am there in the midst of them."* (Matthew 18:20 NKJV). So in consonance with the previous chapters that discuss finding accountability and leveraging wise counsel, you can also find safety and a group of like-minded believers who will pray with you and help you reach your financial goals.

By now, you may be catching on to the self-evaluation journey and how these activities are solidified through journaling and documentation. Journaling your prayer requests and their answers allows you to see how God moves on your behalf and builds faith to continue the practice. It's important to include that practical step because we often pray, ask God for something, and forget that he gave it to us. But if you write down the prayer request, you can also celebrate when God answers those prayer requests. I like to write down my prayer requests. Consider reviewing your prayer requests and their answers in a group setting; it allows others to celebrate and praise God with you when He answers our prayers.

Brandon and Tanya crafted an innovative way to mark their wins. They possessed $225,000 of debt, with each individual debt ranging between $1,000 - $20,000. They sought wise counsel and developed a plan that included adjusting their spending behaviors and living on one income to methodically eliminate their debt. They drafted a chart of debtors that included defined milestones. Then, they outlined how they would celebrate their progress as they reached each milestone.

Brandon and Tanya are "foodies" and wanted to explore local restaurants. Their celebration milestones included identifying one new restaurant per milestone—they would dine at a new restaurant as their celebration activity. Since they had multiple debts they needed to pay off, it meant lots of restaurants to visit.

Although this example may seem like a small celebration, it motivated them to continue working toward their ultimate goal. Break your petitions to God into small segments, and celebrate incremental progress. Even the most daunting tasks can be accomplished gradually over time.

Building up the practice of regular conversations with God helps us to transition our mindset from a position of self-control to a posture of allowing God to design and structure our path. When we maintain control of our situations, we exclude God. He ALWAYS has a better solution. His outcomes are better than what we could have imagined for ourselves. In an earlier chapter, you identified your habits and behaviors and determined that there are some things you could be doing better (self-examination). Now you know exactly what you can pray about. Completely release these petitions to God.

Pray and then move as God directs you to move. Include prayers for stewardship and financial knowledge in your devotional time. Philippians 4:6 says, *"Be anxious for nothing, but in everything by prayer and supplication, with thanksgiving, let your requests be made known to God."* When God moves, celebrate the wins.

Successful Prayer and Self-Examination include:

1. Surrendering your finances to God.
2. Asking God to grant the desires of your heart, which includes writing down your prayer requests and the answers to your prayers.
   a. If you don't know the issues of your heart, ask God to reveal them to you. Give your heart issues a name so you can begin your healing.
3. Celebrating your wins.
4. Not becoming discouraged if God's answer is delayed. Remember that God has plans for you and always wants to see you prosper (Jeremiah 29:11-13), so choose joy in the waiting.

LESSON: When we give our control to God, He crafts better outcomes than we could have imagined ourselves.

Visit our website and download a copy of the ***Powerful Prayers*** template. The template guides you through 1 Corinthians 29:11-12. This scripture passage is a framework that starts with acknowledging that God knows everything and controls the power, recognition, financial prosperity, and everything in between. These acknowledgments prepare your heart to petition Him. The template allows you to record your prayers and your progress. Remember, when God answers, don't forget to give Him personal praise!

BIBLE REFERENCE AND REFLECTION:

Jeremiah 29:11-13 NKJV

[11] For I know the thoughts that I think toward you, says the Lord, thoughts of peace and not of evil, to give you a future and a hope. [12] Then you will call upon Me and go and pray to Me, and I will listen to you. [13] And you will seek Me and find Me, when you search for Me with all your heart.

"There is only one way to eat an elephant: a bite at a time."

– Desmond Tutu

CHAPTER

6

STRIKING DOWN
STRONGHOLDS

FINANCIAL DECISIONS ARE
SPIRITUAL DECISIONS.

A spiritual stronghold is a lie or a false narrative that Satan has established within our thinking that we hold as truth. It is counterproductive to the behaviors that we want to have. Strongholds change our attitudes, our emotions, and or our behaviors. We can fall short of reaching our full potential without wrangling our strongholds into submission.

Strongholds will materialize as opinions, assumptions, misinterpretations, and unhealthy spending habits. So when you have a stronghold, you must acknowledge that you have it, seek help, and then intentionally plan to walk in victory every day. Examples of strongholds include fear, guilt, worry, trust, contentment, anger, identity, pride, and idolatry.

If you are unable to make wise financial decisions, it may be rooted in a lack of overall subject knowledge. If you find it difficult to make confident, assertive financial decisions, the root cause may be fear. If you impulsively spend money in one or more areas, you may be dealing with an addiction. If you struggle to achieve true satisfaction with your financial status, this is likely a contentment issue. You could be experiencing multiple spiritual challenges at one time.

Another common stronghold is the poverty mentality or poverty mindset. People possessing the poverty mindset believe they will never have enough money to satisfy their needs and wants. When this thought is prominent (whether conscious or unconscious), people either:

- Spend all the money that comes through their hands with the underlying thought that this type of financial injection will not happen again, otherwise known as "you only live once" (YOLO), or
- Save everything they get with the same underlying reasoning.

Neither of these extremes is healthy because they don't consider God's blessings or future progression; it typically keeps you in cyclical behaviors.

One of my strongholds is worry. Worry was beginning to consume my thoughts throughout the day. I was constantly creating "what if" scenarios and calculating how to fix something that hadn't even happened. It was mentally exhausting, and I needed to turn this over to God. I can indeed be stubborn, so I pulled out the full-proof plan—implementing a fasting routine. Every Saturday evening at midnight, I began a 12-hour fast of food, drink, social media, and other forms of entertainment. I fast, pray, and ask God to keep me from worrying. I give my issues over to God to help me have peace in my life. Whenever I let go of the worry, it allows me to focus on more positive things. God will take care of our needs and provide for us because He is our Jehovah Jireh (provider), and we just have to trust him to be there.

Typically, a fast is for a finite amount of time. However, I never want to take this issue lightly, so I maintain the routine. Fasting should remove anything (within your power) that can interrupt or counteract what God is trying to say to me during that time. The activity also includes finding a quiet space for meditation and engaging in a mentally and physically receiving posture. I allow him to continue healing me from that stronghold and other strongholds not explicitly mentioned here.

Like an addiction, a stronghold is something you must acknowledge and work on daily. If you do not, it can overtake your financial decision. We need to acknowledge the spiritual component of our decisions. We have to understand what our strongholds are. If you're unsure of your strongholds, ask people you trust—your friends and family, who share the same spaces with you—to reveal the spiritual or financial challenges they see in you. Then, open yourself up to God's revelation.

To begin healing:

1. Identify your strongholds. Deploy to the assistance of those who know you well, if needed.

2. Briefly journal about those things (say five minutes a day), and over time, you'll be able to recognize patterns that you tend to repeat.

   a. The journaling should include how you feel about the patterns and behaviors. Returning to a previous example on impulsive spending, write down how you feel about purchasing. Does the purchase make you happy or anxious? Are you excited, etc.?

   b. Document your feelings surrounding purchases you do not need. Go a step further and document your thoughts on making any purchase—paying the utility bill, the expense of having lunch with a friend, or whatever purchases you intend to make that day. Apply this type of exploration to whatever stronghold applies to you.

   c. You'll begin accumulating information allowing you to review what you've written.

3. Look for repeating themes. The identified themes may or may not benefit you, but note any unhealthy patterns you recognize; these are likely strongholds.

4. Change your language. There are often counteractive verses or affirmation statements that can be leveraged to begin the journey of moving away from those strongholds.

Your current financial situation combines how you've been nurtured, everything you've learned, and everything you've done over the years. Some of these things are counterproductive to your financial journey. To change your financial situation, you have to change what you believe, and your changes will be reflected in what you do. Moreover, the scriptures will help you combat your flesh and your fears.

Multiple scriptures govern my life—scriptures that remind me that God owns everything, that remind me that prosperity is gained over time, that remind me to not worry about tomorrow, and that remind me that debt is slavery. Digesting these scriptures builds your muscle and combats your flesh and your fears. When you know that God will take care of you, you can begin to focus on Him and let him control the situations around you.

LESSON: Financial decisions are spiritual decisions.

Take our ***Identifying Strongholds*** quiz and start addressing areas of your life where your internal belief system needs to change.

BIBLE REFERENCES AND REFLECTIONS:

2 Timothy 1:7 NKJV

For God has not given us a spirit of fear, but of power and of love and of a sound mind.

James 1:5 NKJV

If any of you lacks wisdom, let him ask of God, who gives to all liberally and without reproach, and it will be given to him.

Philippians 4:11-12 NIV

[11] *I am not saying this because I am in need, for I have learned to be content whatever the circumstances. [12] I know what it is to be in need, and I know what it is to have plenty. I have learned the secret of being content in any and every situation, whether well-fed or hungry, whether living in plenty or in want.*

CHAPTER

7

TRACK YOUR EXPENSES

DETERMINE THE BUDGETING PROCESS
THAT BEST SUITS YOUR PERSONALITY AND
WILL ENABLE YOUR SUCCESS.

The "B" word is something many people shy away from. If you're in that camp, prayerfully, I can make the concept seem more doable because if you ever want to become debt-free, you must have a **B**udget. Consider your budget as a series of jars you repeatedly fill, pour out, and refill. When your income presents itself, you fill the jars. When you pay your bills or make purchases, you pour out of those respective jars. Then when additional income presents itself, refill your jars. For the discussions in this content, let's assume the cycle is monthly or that we are working to create and maintain a monthly budget.

Do you know your income and expenses, and do you ensure that you allocate funds to satisfy all of your expenses? Income, expenses, and allocation are the foundational components of a zero-based budget. A zero-based budget is when a plan has been made to allocate all your income, usually by expense categories. Common spending categories include Housing, Food, Transportation, and Medical. Other frequently used categories are entertainment, clothing, savings/investing, debt repayment, and miscellaneous. If you have children, you may also have a category for their spending. No matter your financial status or family situation, there should be no income that doesn't have an assignment.

If you're fortunate to make more than what you spend each month, then assigning a name to every dollar could include higher allocations to debt repayments, savings, or investing. If you're making less than your monthly expenses, assigning every dollar is crucial and strategic to remain afloat. When assigning every dollar to a category, there may be spending categories you cannot fund (maybe your entertainment category, for example). After you've allocated your funds, any unfunded categories should remain visible to reflect your desire to allocate funds to that category at some point in the future. When you reach a point where you have given every dollar a name AND you can adequately fund every applicable spending category, you will have a zero-based, fully-funded budget.

Suppose you are unfamiliar with building a budget or require more explanation on these concepts. In that case, I recommend you schedule an appointment with a budget coach or similar resource to step you through the process, which begins with tracking and categorizing your spending. You will need a record of all your spending within a certain period, including bank statements, receipts, or digital communications. Once you've collected sufficient spending records, organize and summarize the information into spending categories. Then, let the empirical evidence highlight your good and/or bad spending patterns. We will further address the analysis of your budget in the next chapter. For now, the focus is to start a new habit of tracking expenses.

To have a working budget, you need to understand when you receive income and when you need to make payments. You need to know whether the payments or obligations that you have come on a regular or an irregular basis. If they are irregular (an expected expense only paid a few times a year), incorporate those amounts into your budget by totaling the expected annual expense and dividing that by 12. Insurance premiums (if your provider has not adapted to a payment plan or regular expenses) are a good example of an irregular expense.

There are also variable expenses (expenses you can anticipate but can't pinpoint the exact value) that must be accounted for in your budget. Utilities, gasoline, and groceries are typically variable expenses because they rely on commodities priced on supply and demand. Stick with me as we switch to the practical side of budgeting.

Practicality in budgeting comes into consideration for summarization and recordkeeping. Are you a person who likes to use paper and pencil? Do you prefer a spreadsheet? Do you prefer an app? All are adequate and possess benefits and challenges related to ease of use, personal data security, and data accuracy. Ultimately, your practical tool of choice should be something you will stick with and develop discipline around because you will have to access that tool, paper, and pencil, app, or spreadsheet regularly.

One of our clients tracked her expenses and created her initial budget in Excel. She thought it would be straightforward to place all her expenses into a spreadsheet and to create formulas that allow the tool to calculate total spending by category and overall. She felt the spreadsheet provided flexibility and was familiar with the tool, so navigation was not a concern. As it turns out, a more automated tool was preferred when adding multiple accounts and dynamic transactions to the equation. It was overwhelming to constantly adjust formulas and formats within the tool to accommodate her spending activities.

This client switched to Quicken, an Intuit product, which came with a small price tag. Transparently, most available apps have a subscription cost, and they may store your banking data somehow. But if you land on the right tool for your lifestyle, tolerance, and budget, the investment will be well worth it as it allows you to create the behaviors necessary to keep you on track.

To solidify the behavior of tracking your expenses, you must anticipate the best way to save your receipts and download information from your bank account. Set aside 30 minutes a week to accomplish this task. It will prevent expenses from building up and ensure you don't have too much information to process and categorize.

LESSON: Determine the budgeting process that best suits your personality and will enable your success. If you try out one tool and determine you have chosen it incorrectly, switching to a different tool is perfectly okay (it's a no-judgment zone).

To build and maintain a successful budget:

1. Create spending categories. There are many standard categories, but relabel or add spending categories to work with your situation.
2. Identify your main method of spending: cash, debit, or credit.
   a. If cash is preferred, you must collect receipts with every purchase.
   b. Choosing a debit or credit card as your primary spending method does not exclude you from collecting receipts, as many retailers sell items from multiple spending categories (i.e., some grocery stores sell gas and food,

and some big box stores provide pharmacy services and household products).

    i. When you purchase items from multiple categories from one retailer, you will need to manually split the overall total by category.

    ii. You must also ensure you can download or export the statements efficiently with debit and credit cards.

3. Pick a tool to help summarize and analyze your financial data.

a. Don't hide or exclude any values. The information will only be beneficial long-term if you're being open, honest, and transparent with your numbers. Don't let guilt or any other issue creep in to prevent you from keeping track of your expenses. You can only accept where you are if you see everything in black and white.

4. Review the data and compare it to your expectations.

Once you can start walking through the required activities to build and maintain a budget, you will find greater discipline, organization, and progress in your finances. Visit our website for links to existing financial tracking and summarization apps or to download and populate your editable ***Budgeting Spreadsheet and Spending Tracker***.

BIBLE REFERENCE AND REFLECTION:

Proverbs 27:23-24 NKJV

[23] *Be diligent to know the state of your flocks, And attend to your herds;* [24] *For riches are not forever, Nor does a crown endure to all generations.*

CHAPTER

8

ANALYZE YOUR SPENDING

ANALYSIS ENABLES MORE ACCURATE
STRATEGIES.

Take a moment to congratulate yourself on deciding that budgeting is an essential part of your financial journey. You may also have needed to shed unproductive thoughts, behaviors, and strongholds to realize this. A budget is impactful because it directly connects you to a detailed plan—intentional actions surrounding your spending. But, what takes the budgeting discipline to a new level is the analysis—a detailed, reactive process that evaluates your recent spending history and allows you to modify future spending deliberately. Here is where you check in on your plan's effectiveness.

Are you meeting your budgeting expectations? Were you in debt when you decided to pivot to this biblical approach? Becoming debt free becomes easier or more difficult to achieve depending on your financial status when you apply these principles. If you are married with children or a low-income earner with student loan debt, without God's grace, your path to financial freedom may seem more daunting than a single, high-income earner with a car loan and credit card debt. Those in the former statuses may need to consider significant lifestyle changes that impact others to make progress. There are likely fewer spending categories to adjust before your family "feels" the difference.

On the other hand, a single, high-income earner could sell their expensive car, stop purchasing new clothes for a few months and become debt free in a short timeframe. The speed of progress and results seen in these two scenarios will likely differ (visit our website to view the *Financial Trajectories* table).

Several factors can determine your financial freedom trajectory, so it is important to not play the comparison game. If you begin comparing your circumstances to others, you will likely have old or new strongholds creep in at this point of your journey. These feelings could stall your progress if not addressed. If you are experiencing this, go back to Chapter 3 and work your way through the healing process again.

To thrive with this framework, you must do something with your data. The first step in analyzing your spending is to set some parameters and baselines about how much you should spend in a certain category. There are many financial professionals who have an opinion on what the parameters should be. Feel free to research your preferred grouping of spending recommendations. Below are suggested spending category allocations that work for most situations. Spend a few minutes pondering and justifying your reference guide; ensure you agree and align with the structure. It is wise to talk through your thoughts about these guidelines with a trusted advisor. In consultation with your budget coach, you may decide that some slight adjustments are needed for your unique situation. The takeaway here is that you stick to these spending references so they can guide your spending decisions. The reference and this process will lose effectiveness if the values do not remain constant.

SPENDING GUIDELINES

CATEGORY	GUIDELINE	COMMENTS
TITHING	10%	While all other category recommendations are derivatives of your net pay, tithing should be calculated as a percentage of your gross pay. Practically speaking (within your budget), this amount will be higher than 10% of your net spending.
HOUSING	20-40%	It is not uncommon for those on the lower end of the income spectrum to trend closer to the higher end of the provided range.
TRANSPORTATION	13-20%	Ideally, vehicles are purchased and managed without incurring debt (or a recurring payment) which would allow an allocation closer to the lower end of the provided range.
HEALTH & WELLNESS	3%	Any expenses related to medical, dental, or vision are included here.
ENTERTAINMENT	3-6%	Allocations will vary based on your obligations and goals.
CLOTHING	3-5%	Allocations will vary based on your individual preferences.
FOOD	6-15%	Dining out is a common activity; decide whether your dining expenses are included here or as part of your entertainment expenses.
MISCELLANEOUS	3-5%	This catch-all category should be minimized (and directed to more specific categories when possible) as expenses landing here will be more difficult to regulate.
SAVINGS/ INVESTING	5%	Invest in yourself; ensure you have funds to cover emergencies, income gaps and large purchases
CREDIT CARDS	0-5%	Credit card debt can impact your freedom to serve God freely, your personal health, your financial reputation, and/or your overall net worth.
CHILDCARE	0-5%	Allocate any and all expenses related to caring for your children's well-being.

You may notice that these percentages do not add up to 100. However, when you analyze your budget, they should add up to 100. Since there are multiple financial scenarios, you may not need one or more categories defined above, or there may need to be a conscious sacrifice made to accomplish a zero-based budget.

Your first round of analysis should include three calculating columns—your actual expenses for a given category, the guideline expense for a given category (from the above table), and your budgeted amount for the same category. There should be enough insight between these three numbers to determine your future strategy and behavior. For example, after tracking your expenses, you have calculated a housing category total of $1,290. You have also determined that your guideline housing expenditures should be 30% of your take-home pay or $1,200 (well within the range provided in the above table). However, you have also recently learned that you can decrease your phone bill by $25 by choosing a different plan and decrease your electricity bill by $25 by adjusting your thermostat. You commit to applying a few behavioral changes, so you decide to set your housing budget amount at $1,240. In this example, previous spending of $1,290 compared with a guideline of $1,200 led to a commitment to spend less in the housing category ($1,240 is closer to the $1,200 guideline). This progress should be celebrated.

You can also be proactive in your commitments. If you set a certain amount for eating out monthly, $200, for example, and you know that your restaurant bills are approximately $50 each time you eat out, you can realistically plan to eat out four times during the month. $200 divided by $50 equals four trips to the restaurant. Knowing exactly what your budget allows enables boundaries and different decisions.

There have been several instances when we've analyzed our spending and realized that we spent more on groceries or more than our budget allows. Once we acknowledged that overspending was not an outlying circumstance but a lack of self-control and planning, we immediately incorporated strategies to realign our actual spending with our budget. These strategies included meal planning, purchasing in bulk, and committing to decreasing trips to the grocery store. If you're not analyzing your spending, you will miss the revelations. Begin routinely looking back at your spending history and ensuring you adhere to your budget.

LESSON: Tracking your expenses (having the data) and analyzing your expenses (doing something with the data) are separate activities. The analysis enables more accurate strategies.

Budget Analyzing Factors:

1. **Reduce the number of opinions you consider**

   Don't listen to too many podcasts, read too many blogs, or watch too many vlogs. They can prevent you from making a definitive choice. Why? Because everybody has a different idea about how to manage money. It is possible to distill these inputs into a framework of your own. But, as you are starting this journey, I recommend choosing an existing framework and limiting your exposure to other ideas until you've reached a point in your journey where a change is needed.

2. **Weekly Schedule**

   Schedule a weekly time to review your bank account and how you spent your money that week. The weekly reviews and check-ins will help you reach your monthly goals because you will be cognizant of whether or not you are over or underspending in particular categories, allowing you to make any needed course corrections.

3. **Avoid the analysis loop**

   Avoid getting stuck in the loop of analysis (also known as analysis paralysis). If a root cause is not obvious, seek out someone who can help you through the process.

4. **Forgive yourself**

   Forgive yourself for past spending mistakes. Forgive yourself for future spending mistakes. Don't allow guilt or shame to creep in if you find yourself overspending again. Move forward and try again, even if you don't execute your budget perfectly. Pray and ask God for strength to continue the race.

   Financial success can only be achieved with discipline over time. Your confidence will grow with repetition—track your spending, analyze it (then do it repeatedly). Repetition builds competence, and competence facilitates success.

   I encourage you to look at your accounts regularly. Open your mobile banking account, and review how you spent your money in the past week. Determine whether you are on track to meet your goals based on your recent spending. Ask yourself, "What changes do I need to make?"

   Update your *Spending Tracker* (originally downloaded in Chapter 7) and capture your insights.

BIBLE REFERENCE AND REFLECTION:

Psalm 121:1-2 NKJV

¹ I will lift up my eyes to the hills—From whence comes my help? ² My help comes from the Lord, Who made heaven and earth.

CHAPTER

9

ADJUST AND ACHIEVE

TO ACHIEVE A DEBT-FREE LIFESTYLE, YOU
MUST BEGIN TO MAKE PURCHASES WITH
CASH EQUIVALENTS.

Hopefully, you are beginning to see that debt freedom is possible. Going through the process of systemically making better lifestyle and spending choices should result in your debts melting away, which is a wonderful byproduct of applying this framework. Deferring certain purchases may not be fun, but you are also now aware that delayed gratification doesn't kill you. Hopefully, you're beginning to lean more on God as your provider and becoming more aware that he rewards obedience and adherence to His word. These are necessary characteristics for sustaining lifelong financial freedom.

When God places His hand in your finances, anything is possible. Checks begin to mysteriously appear in the mailbox, debt forgiveness appears without prompting, and new income opportunities present themselves right on time. God can accelerate any timeline, change anyone's financial circumstances, and upgrade anyone's lifestyle. He only wants to ensure your motivations are pure – that you are ultimately focused on impacting the kingdom.

Here is a true story. We were in the market for a fairly used (but new to us) vehicle that could support our family dynamics for multiple seasons. After identifying a few vehicle options from an internet search, we were ready to inspect and test drive the vehicle in person. We arrived at the dealership and requested a test drive of the advertised vehicle. Here's where the bait and switch started. The salesperson indicated the vehicle we wanted to see would take some time to retrieve (several cars were blocking it) and directed our attention to a "similar vehicle." As I inspected the vehicle's exterior, I noticed the sticker price was $7,000 over our budget, but we went ahead with the test drive because, well, the salesperson recommended it (shrug). We didn't want to waste time or inconvenience anyone by having our requested vehicle pulled around. I can still remember how nice the vehicle's interior was—all the bells and whistles, seats like butter, and a suspension gliding down the road. All the features and functionality were impressive, so we began rationalizing how to make this purchase work—we could use more savings or find a way to finance the purchase. This is a trick of the enemy. It is a trick that gets us right where the devil wants us, justifying living beyond our means and not walking in contentment.

Within a few minutes, our heads were back in the game. We refocused and politely declined to purchase this vehicle. It would have been easy to finance and drive that vehicle off the lot. But we remained committed to our financial plan and kept looking until we found the right vehicle within our price range, one we could pay for with cash. As a silver lining, the vehicle we purchased is also eye-catching, comfortable, and impressive in its own right. Often, we think contentment leads us down a boring, unfulfilling path where we are no longer proud and confident of our purchased possessions. Don't believe that! You can lead a confident, fulfilled, content life with adjusted behaviors.

In Chapter 8, we talked about course corrections and how it is necessary to make an immediate adjustment when you notice that you're overspending in a particular category. This chapter will provide a deep dive into additional proactive strategies.

1. **Using Cash or cash equivalents for all purchases**

   Cash is King. Using cash or cash equivalents for all purchases takes discipline but facilitates freedom. In today's world, almost all of us have access to credit. However, if you behave as if credit is not an option (or you use cash to make all your purchases), then when the money is depleted, the spending must cease until additional money is gained.

Adjusting to cash purchases impacts your ability to overspend because the ability to access nebulous funds is removed from the equation. Use cash for your purchases whenever possible, even if it means delaying the purchase until you've adequately saved the funds. You'll have a greater appreciation for the purchase, and it will prevent debt from becoming a curse in your life.

2. **Moving funds from another spending category**

   Remember that flexibility in your budget and spending categories is encouraged as long as the adjustments do not occur regularly. This strategy is valid when it is possible to delay a purchase to allow space for a more urgent need. Let's say I have been given an opportunity to go on a vacation with friends and family in a few months but haven't budgeted for this expense. I might still be able to go on this trip if I make temporary sacrifices in other spending categories. I have followed the recommended spending guidelines in my fully-funded budget and have planned spending amounts for the clothing and food (specifically eating out) categories. However, while I enjoy purchasing new clothing and eating out, I can temporarily limit or exclude these activities from my lifestyle to redirect funds to my travel budget. This is a great strategy to deploy when we can be disciplined enough to remember that a temporary change has been made in our budget.

3. **Walking away from the purchase**

This is the hardest option to execute unless we have a strong purpose and goals motivating our desires elsewhere. When you strongly desire something or if you see a great deal (i.e., something on clearance that won't be available again in the near future), walking away from the purchase could produce some strong feelings or sentiments. Implementing this strategy hasn't yet become "easy" for me. Still, it is doable because I remind myself that I have committed to something greater and that God will see and honor my obedience.

4. **Preparing in advance for purchases (Saving)**

Life happens, and you will want to set yourself up for success, ensuring that a few financial storms won't knock you down or that you won't consider debt an option. When we're willing to invest the time, we can predict future expenses and prevent future debt. Our prediction barometer may vary, but the idea is to prepare for surprises (sounds crazy, right). Saving is a mandatory element of achieving financial stability.

There are four progressive saving categories; emergency, living expenses, holding accounts, and retirement. Save for emergencies first, then move on to income replacement to shield yourself from short-term downfalls. Once you fully fund your emergency and living expenses, focus on more proactive savings vehicles, holding accounts, and retirement savings.

All savings categories should be given proper respect and energy, but complete these milestones to ensure accessibility. For example, there is an imbalance if you heavily contribute to your retirement account(s) but struggle to pay for a car repair. Visit my website and download the ***Progressive Savings*** guide, a deep dive into each savings type with examples.

5. **Moving funds from your savings account**

   Withdrawing money from your savings account is a form of spending. Generally, funds in a savings account are reserved for a specific purpose. However, when funds are needed for an unplanned purchase, it can be acceptable to utilize your savings (as long as you're disciplined enough to replace the funds). Let's say I've done the work in previous chapters and have budgeted for car maintenance based on my last few trips to the mechanic, but I've just been informed that

I need a separate service at a separate cost. Most of us would be tempted to overspend or utilize credit in this scenario because our vehicles are usually attached to something important (transportation to work, the doctor, or to church). Instead, using funds from your savings account can fill the gap when shortfalls occur, and you can avoid overspending.

LESSON: To achieve a debt-free lifestyle, you must begin to make purchases with cash equivalents.

The adjustments just mentioned will help you achieve a life without debt. You must learn to pay for all your purchases with money you can allocate from your budget. You can't keep doing the same thing, or you'll get the same results. You must be willing to change how you do things to maintain discipline, which may mean making difficult decisions.

Spending Behavior Adjustments:

1. Expose yourself to fewer advertisements because advertisers can pull you in. That's their job—to make something enticing to you. Avoiding enticement helps to prevent the purchase decision or consideration.

2. Create a fully funded budget, not just a zero-based budget. While it is admirable to not spend more than you make, making space for other prudent purchases is next level.

3. Make saving a priority (Proverbs 21:20).

4. Don't compare your lifestyle to anyone else's. Sometimes people get discouraged because they compare their lifestyles to others. People's needs vary based on their lifestyle, their current family life, their current career structure, and their current marital status. So many factors explain why someone may be experiencing a certain financial situation. Don't compare; rather, ask God to bless you in your situation.

Finally, finalize what you've uncovered during your analysis. Talk to your counselor or accountability partner and begin to put these things into practice. To prepare for the future, especially now that you understand how God has called you to be impactful, I encourage you to embrace this awareness and understand what legacy you will leave. Your legacy intentions should determine how you allocate your income. Once you have a stable financial status, you must determine how to monetize your goals and leverage them appropriately to impact God's kingdom.

BIBLE REFERENCE AND REFLECTION:

I Corinthians 3: 9-11 NIV

[9] *For we are co-workers in God's service; you are God's field, God's building.* [10] *By the grace God has given me, I laid a foundation as a wise builder, and someone else is building on it. But each one should build with care.* [11] *For no one can lay any foundation other than the one already laid, which is Jesus Christ.*

CHAPTER

10

PREPARING FOR THE FUTURE

BUILDING WEALTH WILL FACILITATE THE
EXECUTION OF YOUR GOALS

We're now at a point where your new behaviors and actions are beginning to show fruit. You've eliminated financial stress by shifting your mindset and incorporating Godly wisdom into everyday activities. Prayerfully, you now have a surplus of funds, and you can further activate your purpose, which could be impacting your immediate family, your community, or your extended community. You have a lot going for you. How will you build on this momentum?

In the first two chapters, your motivation and short goals may have been colored by your financial circumstances. Now, we want to remove limitations and broaden your significance. Consider the following questions:

1. What do you want to see in the world?
2. Which of your long-term commitments or responsibilities have a financial component?
3. Who depends on you for their well-being?
4. Do you support your children or parents in any way?
5. What type of leisure or entertainment activities do you enjoy?
6. How many homes should you own?
7. How many vehicles do you want/need?

8. Do you desire advanced education (certificates or degrees)?
9. What charities or causes do you support?
10. Do you plan to work until age 62? Will your retirement savings support you after age 62?

As you respond to these questions, add any new insights to your goals template (from Chapter 2). Your revised list of items may require saving tens of thousands of dollars. It may be time to activate an investment strategy where you can generate passive income to fund your future goals. Building wealth will facilitate the execution of your goals because money as a tool can enable great things. We can passively build wealth through real estate, buying and selling stocks and bonds, creating a small business, or investing in fine art (just to name a few).

Real estate investments may come in the form of an inheritance or transfer of ownership. If you experience this type of wealth transfer, consider holding the property long-term. Real estate is still a mostly safe, mostly appreciating asset. Property is also a limited commodity. While I've seen savvy business people turn single occupancy dwellings into multiple occupancy dwellings, the United States of America has not acquired any more states or territories in quite some time. From my point of view, this means that if you own or have the opportunity to own property and said property is/ can produce positive cash flow, you should keep it. If it's impossible to keep, consider placing the proceeds into one of the other wealth-generating options mentioned above.

Should you decide to invest in the stock market, I recommend buying and holding smart investments. This strategy aligns with the biblical principle of steady plodding (Proverbs 21:5). When we consider our investments as all short-term opportunities, it often changes our perspective on who controls our increase (1 Chronicles 29:11-12). The Lord frowns upon gambling, and too much risky financial behavior, including day trading or house flipping, can lead to the wrong mentality for the average person. Typical behavior includes obsessing and stressing over the outcome of these investments because it could result in a significant increase or decrease. To be clear, this is not a condemnation of calculated risk-taking nor a condemnation of having fun. It is, however, a reminder that too much risk can lead to too much dependence on ourselves (when we should depend on God).

LESSON: As you choose your investments, weigh them alongside your long-term goals.

Include the following activities when preparing for your future:

1. Buy and hold smart investments. This will generate income for you all the time and make your life less stressful because your money will be doing the work for you.

2. Be attentive to and invest in circumstances that require a compassionate spirit to advance. Activate your purpose.

3. Steward your money in a way that will benefit you and those coming behind you.

If God has blessed you financially, he wants you to be generous to others (Luke 16:10). Be someone who God can trust with more. Show Him that you can handle abundance. Update your ***Goal Planning*** template to include a 10-year timeline.

BIBLE REFERENCES AND REFLECTIONS:

Proverbs 21:5 TLB

"Steady plodding brings prosperity; hasty speculation brings poverty."

Luke 16:10-11 NIV

[10] *"Whoever can be trusted with very little can also be trusted with much, and whoever is dishonest with very little will also be dishonest with much.* [11] *So if you have not been trustworthy in handling worldly wealth, who will trust you with true riches?"*

EPILOGUE

Now that you've identified the root of your financial challenges and uncovered your greater purpose, you can sustain more effective financial strategies. There is no longer a reason to remain stuck in an unproductive cycle. Use your tools to change your trajectory and shed the weight of regretful financial decisions. Take off the poverty mindset veil and experience confidence and joy.

In this book, you have learned strategies that will help you shift your mindset, build your spiritual muscle, and make better financial decisions.

Chapter 1: Define Your Why clearly identifies the inspiration and drive behind your actions. Your why is a litmus test that helps to distinguish your priorities.

Chapter 2: Goal Planning leads to progress and results. This intentional activity will provide focus when multiple things are competing for your attention.

Chapter 3: Evaluate Your Habits, Your Personality, and Tendencies provides transparency to your opportunity areas. You can't fix what you won't first acknowledge. So, it is important to "do the work" that identifies the specific petitions that you will release into God's capable hands.

Chapter 4: Discipline and Financial Discipleship underscores the importance of looking outside yourself for answers. Godly counsel is priceless. It can help you avoid making decisions that will require significant effort to correct.

Chapter 5: Prayer and Personal Examination ensures you don't forget who controls everything. Your recognition and submission to God's power and ability will bring solutions and resolutions beyond what you envisioned.

Chapter 6: Striking Down Strongholds reminds us that healing and spiritual maturity are important in our financial journey. Reshaping your financial lens will allow you to build and exhibit healthy behaviors that will impact you and those around you.

Chapter 7: Track Your Expenses builds the discipline necessary to sustain victory in your finances. Ensuring that every expense and income vehicle is considered will facilitate building a strong financial strategy.

Chapter 8: Analyze Your Spending moves your tracking from a task to an educational tool. As you identify your successes and setbacks during each budget cycle, you evaluate to build better habits instead of condemning your previous choices.

Chapter 9: Adjust and Achieve creates a check and balances atmosphere. After you've evaluated a previous decision, you also confirm whether that decision aligns with your purpose and goals. When there is parity, double down on the behavior. When there is variance, be flexible to try another strategy.

Chapter 10: Preparing for the Future substantiates our role as a disciple. We ensure that we have explored multiple ways to stabilize and leverage our excess funds. What a joy it is to positively impact God's kingdom.

Don't let this book be the end of your journey. Move forward and live boldly. Continue to ideate and enhance your financial strategies. Share these principles with others so they can also enjoy financial success.

VALUABLE RESOURCES AND TOOLS

Access The Money PSA Library at https://www.hersequoiaconsulting.com and download the following:

PERSPECTIVE Templates

Define Your Why

Goal Planning

Spending Behavior Matrix

Schedule Your Consultation Checklist

SPIRIT Templates

Powerful Prayers

Identifying Strongholds

ACTIONS Templates

Budgeting Apps / Budgeting Spreadsheet

Financial Trajectories

Spending Tracker

Progressive Savings

ABOUT THE AUTHOR

Maya McNeese-Hargett is a consultant and biblical financial coach. With 10 years of teaching and coaching experience, Maya can break down and build back up the most challenging financial situations and has been called to share her insights with the world. Maya lives in Marietta, Georgia, with her husband and daughter. Reach out to her when you are ready to gain victory in your finances by applying Godly principles.

For more information, visit
https://www.hersequoiaconsulting.com.